MW01174262

5·06

Tracy Lonsbey

# Princess in the Pantry

## A guide to cooking, entertaining, and party planning

Tracey Tonsberg

authorHOUSE™

*1663 LIBERTY DRIVE, SUITE 200*
*BLOOMINGTON, INDIANA 47403*
*(800) 839-8640*
*WWW.AUTHORHOUSE.COM*

*AuthorHouse™*
*1663 Liberty Drive, Suite 200*
*Bloomington, IN 47403*
*www.authorhouse.com*
*Phone: 1-800-839-8640*

*AuthorHouse™ UK Ltd.*
*500 Avebury Boulevard*
*Central Milton Keynes, MK9 2BE*
*www.authorhouse.co.uk*
*Phone: 08001974150*

*First published by AuthorHouse 2/2/2006*

*ISBN: 1-4259-0739-3 (sc)*
*ISBN: 1-4259-0740-7 (dj)*

*Printed in the United States of America*
*Bloomington, Indiana*
*Library of Congress Control Number: 2006900183*
*This book is printed on acid-free paper.*

# Inspiration: A product of your creative thinking and work.

Many people have "inspired" me to write this book and have supported me throughout the process. I'll start with one of my best friends, Lisa, who — shall we say —is "challenged" in the kitchen but, she gets an "A" for effort!

She, along with many of my other very good friends, will benefit greatly from this book and I thank all of you for creating a need for it.

Most of the recipes in this book belong to my mother, Marilyn. I have enhanced a few and added a few courses to some of the menus, but she gets all the credit for my favorites and soon to be yours. Thank you, Mom. I love you, and your cooking!

In the past four-and-a-half years, my husband, Kevin, and I have hosted many, many parties. Holidays, wine tastings, fall balls, spring flings, birthdays, christenings, luaus, cocktail parties, dinner parties, etc. I could not have hosted any of these events without his help. He can make everything in the book and truly enjoys being in the kitchen. We have been a team from the beginning and I hope that never changes. He has supported me every step of the way, encouraging me to do this. I love you to pieces, Kevin! Thank you!

Olivia, Alexandra, and Caroline: I love you all very, very much. I hope you'll enjoy this book when you are old enough to read it. I also hope you learn every recipe so that you can take turns having Mommy and Daddy over all the time!

# Table of Contents

# "Must-haves" for your kitchen

# (especially if you're using this book)

"Good" garlic press
Mandoline (or food slicer)
Food processor
"Good" knives:
       *paring knife
       *carving knife
       *bread slicer
Soup crocks with saucers
Electric Mixer
Stainless steel mixing bowls
Galvanized bucket(s)
Serving platters
Serving bowls
Three-tier servers
Lemon bags
Cheese slicer
Pepper mill
Kosher sea salt
Electric frying pan
Fancy toothpicks
Meat pounder
Doilies
Non-stick cookie sheets
Ice bucket with scoop
Assorted baskets
Vegetable steamer
Pastry brush
Egg poacher

# Dinner Party Timeline & Checklist (Sample)

Party date    June 6th
\# of guests    8
Arrival time:    7:30
Dinner time:    8:30

| Menu | Dinner Party #1 | | |
|---|---|---|---|
| **Appetizers:** | | | |
| Time: | 7:00 | | Cheese & Fruit Platter, Hummus and Pita Bread |
| | 6:50 | 7:30 | Spinach Dip with Tortilla Chips |
| | 7:00 | 7:25 | Stuffed Mushrooms |
| **Main Course:** | | | |
| Time: | 7:15 | 8:00 | Heat up the soup, set aside the croutons and cheese |
| | 8:05 | 8:08 | Soup in broiler to melt the cheese, serve |
| | 7:55 | 8:00 | Toss the salad and add cheese and croutons |
| | 7:35 | 8:15 | Twice-baked potatoes on 375° |
| | 6:50 | 8:10 | Tenderloin in oven (350°) |
| | 8:10 | 8:25 | Steam the carrots (stove) |
| | 8:25 | *** | Cut the meat, place on serving platter |

| | | |
|---|---|---|
| 8:30 | *** | Serve the dinner |
| 9:00 | 9:25 | Shortcake in oven |
| 9:15 | 9:20 | Make the whipped cream |

Notes:

*Don't forget the mint leaves as garnish on the strawberry shortcake.

*Did you remember to thaw out the strawberries and cut the fresh ones?

*Put the coffee on at 9:20, to serve with dessert.

# Hosting your First Thanksgiving Dinner

*Roasting a Turkey

*Turkey Stuffing

*Butternut Squash

*Mashed Potatoes

*Creamed Onions

*Carrots

*Peas

*Sweet Potatoes

*Cranberry - Raspberry Relish

*Chocolate Cream Pie

# Roasting a Turkey

Preheat the oven to 325° F.

Remove the neck and giblets from the cavity and then wash the bird inside and out with cold water and pat dry.

Rub the bird inside and outside with a mixture of 1 C. melted butter and ½ tsp. of kosher salt, ¼ tsp. of Bells Seasoning®, and a pinch of white pepper.

Place the turkey — breast side up — in a shallow roasting pan on a rack. Cover loosely with aluminum foil to keep the bird moist. At this time, place the stuffing in a covered casserole dish and bake alongside the roast. I do not recommend cooking the stuffing in the cavity of the bird from the start, for food and safety reasons.

Follow the timetable below. One hour prior to the end of the roasting time, remove the foil and baste the bird with the remaining butter mixture. At this time, you can fill the cavity with the cooked stuffing.

The turkey is done when you get an eternal temperature of 165° to 175° F (use a meat thermometer in the thickest part of the breast and the thigh to get an accurate internal temperature reading). At this point, the juices will run clear, not pink.

Cover with foil and let stand 20-30 minutes before carving.

# TIME TABLE

| WEIGHT | TIME |
|---|---|
| 8-12 pounds | 2-3/4 to 3 hours |
| 12-14 pounds | 3 to 3-3/4 hours |
| 14-18 pounds | 3-3/4 to 4-1/4 hours |
| 18-20 pounds | 4-1/4 to 4-1/2 hours |
| 20-24 pounds | 4-1/2 to 5 hours |
| 24+ pounds | 5 to 7 hours |

# Turkey Stuffing

2 large loaves of stuffing bread
3 medium onions (chopped in a food processor)
1½ sticks butter
2 stalks of celery (chopped into small pieces)
2 large eggs (slightly beaten)
1½ C. milk
Bells Seasoning®
Salt and pepper

In a very large bowl, "rip" the stuffing bread into small pieces and let it sit for a few hours or overnight. In a large skillet, melt butter on medium heat and sauté chopped onions and celery until soft (make sure you add some salt and pepper while they are cooking). They will cook for about 15-20 minutes. When they are done, add the onions and celery to your bread. Mix well and add 2 eggs, beaten with the milk. Mix again and sprinkle generously with Bells Seasoning®. Keep mixing until all the bread is moist and it sticks together like a big ball. Add some more salt and pepper. Take your stuffing and put it in a large casserole dish until ready for baking.

Note: You can make the stuffing the day before Thanksgiving to save time.

# Butternut Squash

2 lbs. peeled butternut squash, cut up into 2-inch pieces
1 stick butter
¾ C. packed brown sugar
1 tsp "real" vanilla extract
Salt & pepper

Boil the squash in a large sauce pot until soft (about 25 minutes). Next, pour the squash into a strainer, and "steam out" the water (about 5 minutes). In a large mixing bowl, mash your squash with a potato masher, and add butter and brown sugar. With an electric mixer, whip the squash until smooth (about 1 or 2 minutes on high). Stir in vanilla, add salt and pepper, and pour into a baking dish.

Bake the squash about 35-40 minutes at 375°.

Note* you can prepare this dish the day before. This makes Thanksgiving easier!

# Mashed Potatoes

12 Idaho potatoes, peeled
2 sticks of salted butter, melted
1 pint of whole milk
Salt & pepper

Boil whole potatoes until tender (about 35 minutes). Drain them in a colander and "steam them out" for about 3 minutes. Return the potatoes to the pot and mash them with a hand masher. Gradually add the butter and milk. Using an electric mixer, whip the potatoes until smooth and creamy. Add desired amount of salt and pepper and cover until serving.

# Creamed Onions

2 lbs. of small, white boiling onions
1 pint of heavy cream
½ stick of butter
4 Tbs. of all-purpose flour

In a large saucepan boil the onions until soft. Drain them in a colander. Once they have cooled down, remove the skins and set the onions aside. (Note: This can be done the night before to save time and stove space. Just make sure you store the cooked onions in an airtight, Tupperware® container so your refrigerator doesn't smell like onions.) In a saucepan, melt the butter on low heat. Gradually add the flour, whisking constantly. Cook the flour for 3-5 minutes, making sure it doesn't burn. Gradually add the cream. Keep stirring and do this until you have a creamy, white sauce. Add salt and pepper and add your cooked onions. Set aside and heat them up right before serving.

# Carrots

2 bags of carrots, peeled
¼ stick of salted butter

Once the carrots have been peeled, cut the tops off. Then, cut them in thirds. Then, cut them in half, lengthwise. Boil them until tender. Toss with butter, salt and pepper, and serve.

# Sweet Potatoes

8 large sweet potatoes
Butter

Wash the potatoes and prick them with a fork a couple times. Bake them in the oven at 400° for 1 hour. If you are limited on oven space, feel free to cook them for 1½ hours with the turkey. You want them to be tender. Split potatoes down the middle and place a pat of butter in each one.

# Sweet Peas

2 15 oz. cans of Le Sueur® Very Young Small Early Peas

Open the cans and pour contents into a medium saucepan and heat. (I know this is an easy one, but, I grew up on these and in my opinion, they're the best!)

# Cranberry/Raspberry Relish

2 pkgs. fresh cranberries (ground)
1 large package of raspberry Jell-O®
2 C. boiling water
1 small can orange juice (thawed)
4 C. sugar
1 can strained crushed pineapple

Grind cranberries in a food processor. Mix raspberry Jell-O®, water, and thawed orange juice together. Next, add the sugar and pineapple and ground cranberries and stir to combine. Let this mixture stand overnight in a large bowl.

Serve your cranberry relish with Thanksgiving dinner.

You may also fill pretty jars with this relish and give it to your good friends as a Happy Thanksgiving gift!

# Chocolate Cream Pie

1 ¼ C. graham cracker crumbs
¼ C. sugar
5 Tbs. melted butter
¼ tsp. ground nutmeg
¼ tsp. ground cinnamon
Combine all the above ingredients in a mixing bowl and firmly pack into a 9" pie plate.
2 boxes of Royal® Cook & Serve Chocolate Pudding
3 ¾ C. whole milk

In a medium saucepan, combine both ingredients and cook at medium heat, constantly stirring until the pudding comes to a full boil. Allow pudding to cool slightly (while still stirring), and pour into the pie shell.

Let the pie sit for about 5 minutes and cover with wax paper, making sure the edges are completely covered with the wax. This will keep your pie from getting "skin."

Refrigerate with the wax paper for at least 2-3 hours.

Cover with homemade whipped cream (page 47)and serve.

# Thanksgiving Notes

# "How to" Host a Holiday Cookie Swap

**One month before the cookie swap:**
Make a list of good friends, family, new neighbors, co-workers, or anyone who you enjoy spending time with. Try to have at least twelve people so that each person goes home with a variety of fresh-baked cookies!

**Three weeks before the cookie swap:**
Send each person an invitation, either professionally done, or created on your computer. I would send the invitations at least three weeks in advance. The holidays are a very busy time of year and people really appreciate advance notice so they can plan for babysitters, etc.

Also, be sure to give yourself ample time to prepare. Ask your guests to RSVP one week prior to the party so you can prepare and not get too stressed out!

Note: If you are having invitations printed at a stationery store, you should check with the printer to see how much lead time is needed.

Include the following directions on your invitation:

Please bring twelve individually wrapped packages of six homemade ("no slice and bakes" allowed) cookies with the recipe attached. You can be very creative packaging your cookies. Have fun!

Note: The number of cookie packages each person brings is dependent on how many people you invite. Twelve people would require each person to bake six dozen cookies. That's about two batches of cookies.

## One week before the cookie swap:

Decide on a festive menu for your guests. If you will be serving alcoholic beverages, you may want to offer a signature drink, along with beer, wine or maybe champagne. Pick up some inexpensive prizes for the winners of the games you play. Some suggestions are scented candles, scratch tickets, movie passes, Starbucks® gift cards, etc. Prepare a shopping list for everything you need, including all your ingredients for your food and whatever paper goods you may need.

## One day before the cookie swap:

Prepare a timeline of what time each appetizer goes into the oven. (Remember, everything should not be out right when your guests arrive, keep a couple new things until about 30-40 minutes after everyone has arrived.) Bake your cookies!!!

# Oatmeal Cookies (Not Your Typical Oatmeal Cookie!)

1 C. butter
1 C. sugar
4 Tbs. milk
1 C. flour
2 C. Quaker Quick Oats®
1 tsp. baking soda

Melt butter and add it to the sugar. Next add milk, flour, baking soda, and quick oats. Mix well and spoon onto non-stick cookie sheets. Bake at 375° for 8-10 minutes. You must check these <u>constantly</u> because they are so thin and buttery, they will burn quickly. Remove from cookie sheet and let them cool on a flat surface. Perfect with a hot cup of tea on a cold snowy day!

# Anise Cookies

1 C. butter (softened)
4 C. flour
1 C. sugar
4 eggs
4 tsp baking powder
4/5 tsp. anise extract

Combine sugar & eggs and beat until light and fluffy. Add butter and mix. Gradually add the flour and baking powder. Next, add the anise extract. Drop by teaspoons onto ungreased cookie sheet. Bake at 350° until the tops are golden brown (10- 12 minutes).

## Icing

2 C. confectioner's sugar
5 Tbs. of milk
Nonpareils

Mix confectioner's sugar with milk. Add the milk gradually. Dip the tops of the cookies into the icing and then dip into the nonpareils.

# Snowball Martini

2 ounces Raspberry Vodka
2 Tbs. Freshly squeezed lemon juice
splash of cranberry juice

Shake well with ice.

Serve in a chilled martini glass rimmed with sugar.

# Fun games we played at the cookie swap

_____

_____

_____

_____

_____

_____

_____

_____

_____

_____

_____

_____

_____

_____

_____

# Cocktail Parties

*Cocktail Party for Forty

*How to Host a Cocktail Party

*How to make a Fruit & Cheese Display

*Shrimp Cocktail

*Vegetable Crudités

*Tenderloin Crostini

*Stuffed Mushrooms

*Mini Reubens

*Mozzarella & Tomato Skewers

*Spinach Dip

* Seared Tuna on Flatbreads with Wasabi

*Scallops Wrapped in Bacon

# Cocktail Party for Forty

## Hors d'oeuvres
Assorted cheeses, crackers, and fruit ✓
Shrimp Cocktail
Spinach Dip with Tortilla Chips ✓
Vegetable Crudités ✓
Stuffed Mushrooms
Tenderloin Crostini
Mini Reubens
Mozzarella & Tomato Skewers
Scallops & Bacon
Scallops & Pineapple
Seared Sesame Tuna on Flatbreads with Wasabi and Arugula

## Beverages/Spirits
Merlot/Cabernet
Chardonnay
Beer
Sparkling Water
Signature Drinks:    Cosmopolitans/Apple Martinis

## What you will need:
Invitations (preferably custom-printed)
Doilies
Ice bucket with scoop
Galvanized bucket
Cocktail napkins
Wine glasses (preferably glass)
Martini glasses
Serving platters (I sometimes use charger plates with doilies)
Music
Fresh flowers and vases
Candles
Lucite frames (optional for featured drink menus)
Cookie sheets (for appetizers)
Ice
Clear, heavy-duty plastic cups (for beer, sparkling water)

# How to Host a Cocktail Party

Pick a date for your party. Decide on a theme, such as an upcoming holiday, spring fling, fall ball, Valentine's Day, etc.)

Send out an invitation with an RSVP date of at least one week prior to your event. Keep in mind that if you are planning on using a stationery store to create do your invitations, you need to allow ample time for printing. Invitations should be sent out four to six weeks before your party.

Decide on a menu of what you will be serving. Cocktail parties generally start at 8:00pm (after dinner). A few passed hors d'oeuvres and a couple of dips or "stationary" items usually work well.

# One week before your party...

Make a list of everyone who will be joining you. Determine the final count of guests.

Make a shopping list of everything you will need at the supermarket, vegetable farm, fish market, butcher, bakery, or wherever you shop for your ingredients.

Make a list of all paper goods, alcoholic beverages, candles, fresh flowers, doilies, music CDs, and everything you will need.

Write out a timeline of when to prepare your appetizers, making sure you give yourself ample time to put it all together. (There is a sample timeline on the next page.)

If you can afford to hire a couple of "helpers" the night of your party, it will be money well spent. It really helps to have someone to hang coats, serve drinks, pass hors d'oeuvres, and help with clean-up.

Don't forget to allow time to clean up or "put a smile on your home" the day of the party. A candle burning in a clean bathroom is a nice touch, as well as arrangements of fresh flowers throughout your home.

# How to make a Fruit and Cheese Platter

After hosting many parties, my husband and I have come up with a few tricks on "how to get them to eat the cheese and crackers." First, it has to look pretty. The way to do this is to add a lot of color and make sure everything is fresh and bite-sized. Secondly, don't slice the cheese: cube it instead. It really works!

1 package of sharp cheddar cheese
1 wedge of "good" blue cheese (Great Hill® is very good!)
1 round of brie
Any seasonal fruit, such as:
Fresh raspberries
Fresh blueberries
Fresh strawberries
Watermelon
Nectarines
Apples
Pomegranates

Select three cheeses and some different fruits and arrange them nicely on a large, tiered platter.

Serve assorted crackers and breads in a basket with a linen napkin placed inside.

You can also dress up your platter or display with fresh flowers or greens draped around your food. Be sure not to use anything poisonous, such as poinsettias!)

Be sure to have spreaders if you're serving hummus and olives.

Be creative and have fun.

# Shrimp Cocktail

3-lb. bag of frozen, peeled, deveined raw shrimp (large, 21-33 ct)
1 C. ketchup
3 Tbs. prepared horseradish
Fresh lemons
3 dashes of Tabasco
Salt & pepper
Romaine lettuce (for garnish)
Crushed ice

In a large stock pot, fill with water 2/3 full. Add about 1tsp. of salt. Bring to a full boil. Add shrimp, and once it comes to a full boil again, it is done. Drain the shrimp in a colander and rinse with cold water to stop additional cooking. Put the shrimp in Tupperware® and refrigerate for at least three hours.

In a bowl, add ketchup and horseradish; mix well. Add 3 dashes of Tabasco and the juice of half a lemon. Salt and pepper to taste. Chill for a couple hours.

Options for serving:

If you are serving this to a group as a stationary hors d'oeuvre, I would use a serving platter or a clamshell dish (Mariposa® or Wilton Armetale® are what I recommend). Spread out clean, dried romaine leaves mostly covering the dish or platter. Use a smaller dish to set on the platter for the cocktail sauce. Spoon on some crushed ice around the lettuce and underneath and put a couple lemons (quartered) around the platter. Add the cold shrimp and serve. Make sure you have toothpicks -- or preferably -- cocktail picks or shrimp forks.

If you are serving this as a first course to an elegant dinner party, I would suggest serving the shrimp in a martini glass for each guest. Arrange some crushed ice at the bottom. Add a lettuce leaf and then "hang" the shrimp around the edge of the glass and put a "dollop" of cocktail sauce in the middle. (You can also put a smaller amount of prepared horseradish next to the cocktail sauce. Then put a small wedge of lemon in there. Your guests will find this very impressive!

# Vegetable Crudités

1 medium red cabbage
1 bag baby carrots
½ lb. of sugar snap peas
2 large green bell peppers
1 pint of cherry tomatoes
3 large cucumbers
2 C. broccoli florets
1 container of sour cream
1 package Hidden Valley Ranch® dip mix
1 head romaine lettuce (garnish)
1 large basket (optional)
1 large, clear plastic bowl, which must fit inside the basket
(optional)

Hollow out the inside of the red cabbage, using a good paring knife and a spoon. (You want it to look like a "cabbage bowl"). Mix the sour cream and Hidden Valley Ranch® dip mix together and refrigerate. Wash all vegetables and set aside into plastic baggies. Wash romaine leaves and store them in baggies as well.

Fifteen minutes before your guests arrive, drape the romaine leaves around the sides or the plastic bowl. Fill the cabbage with the dip mix and place it in the middle. Now take the cut veggies and place them in sections around the cabbage. Place the bowl inside of the basket (if you are using one). If there is space between, on the corners, tuck in a linen napkin on each corner and drape it over the side. If you are serving this at a holiday party, be sure to use red, green (or other festively colored) napkins to keep the theme going.

# Tenderloin Crostini

2 lbs. tenderloin, trimmed
1 loaf French bread
Olive oil
Prepared horseradish
Chives
1 lemon
Boursin cheese spread
Salt and pepper
5 Tbs. sour cream

Roast the tenderloin for 45 min at 350°. While the beef is roasting, cut the French bread into ½" slices. Lightly brush both sides with olive oil and broil for 2 minutes on each side, or just until they are lightly browned. In a bowl, add sour cream, chives, prepared horseradish, a squeeze of lemon, and salt and pepper to taste. Mix well. Once the tenderloin is done, let it sit for 10 minutes and then slice into ¼" slices. Spread a thin layer of Boursin cheese on each crostini, then a slice of beef, and top it with ½ tsp. of horseradish cream sauce. These are a wonderful appetizer and very filling.

# Stuffed Mushrooms

3 pkgs. of very white, medium-sized mushrooms
1 stick of butter
¼ C. of white wine
3 cloves of garlic
2 sleeves of Ritz® crackers
1 medium onion
3 Tbs. of fresh parsley, chopped fine
Parmesan cheese
In a colander, wash all the mushrooms, and gently remove the stems. Make sure the stems are washed thoroughly, because you will be using them in the stuffing.

In a food processor, finely chop the onions, parsley, Ritz® crackers, and mushroom stems **separately** and put aside, in four separate bowls.

In a large skillet, melt the butter. Once the butter is melted, add the onions and sauté on low heat. Mince the garlic in a garlic press and add it to the onion and butter. Keep stirring and cook slowly. Once the onions are soft and they start to brown, add the wine. Next, add the mushroom stems. Keep cooking for about 15 minutes. Add salt and pepper and start to gradually add the Ritz® crumbs. Be careful not to add too many crumbs or the stuffing will be dry. You want to add enough so the stuffing will just stay together in a ball.

Take the clean, dry (pat them dry with a paper towel) mushroom caps and stuff them with a teaspoon. Once all the mushrooms are stuffed, I dip them in a mixture of parmesan cheese mixed with a little bit of Ritz® crumbs.

Bake the mushrooms at 350° for about 20-25 minutes or until nicely browned.

# Mini Reubens

1 package of party rye
1 can of sauerkraut (drained)
½ lb. of baby Swiss cheese
½ lb. of lean corned beef (deli counter)
1 C. Russian dressing

On a cookie sheet, place the mini rye in rows. Cut the corned beef into 2" x 2" pieces. Do the same with the Swiss cheese. On each piece of rye, put a piece of corned beef, then a teaspoon of sauerkraut, a teaspoon of Russian dressing, and a piece of Swiss.

Bake these in the oven at 375° for about 12 minutes, or until the cheese is melted.

Serve hot!

# Mozzarella and Tomato Hors d'oeuvres

Long, fancy toothpicks (the ones with the colored cellophane at the top)
1 container of mozzarella balls (the small ones)
1 pint of cocktail tomatoes
Fresh basil
Olive oil
Balsamic vinegar

On each toothpick, put a mozzarella ball, a tomato, mozzarella ball, and another tomato.

Carefully arrange them on a platter. Arrange some washed basil leaves in between and around. Drizzle with olive oil and a splash of balsamic vinegar and serve.

# Spinach Dip

1 package frozen chopped spinach
1 16-oz package cream cheese
1 can Ro-tel® drained diced tomatoes with green chilies
2 C. shredded Monterey jack cheese
¼ C. heavy cream

Cook and drain spinach thoroughly.

In a casserole dish, add cream cheese and spinach, and mix together. Add Ro-tel® tomatoes and heavy cream. Finally, add the Monterey jack cheese.

Bake at 400° for 35-40 minutes and stir occasionally. Dip is ready when it's hot and bubbly.

Serve with tortilla chips and/or carrots and celery sticks.

# Scallops & Bacon

2 lb. of fresh sea scallops, washed, drained, and cut in half
1-lb. package of lean bacon
Toothpicks

Take the whole package of bacon and cut the bacon in half, lengthwise. Roll one half of a sea scallop with each half piece of bacon. Stick a toothpick in each one, to secure the ends of the bacon to the scallop, and place it on a cookie sheet.

Bake them in the oven at 375° for about 40 minutes. Check them every 10 minutes and turn them.

Tip: You can cook these prior to your cocktail party and just heat them up before your guests arrive. It is a good idea to do this because you probably don't want your kitchen to smell like scallops. To reheat them, cook at 350° for 10 minutes. Serve hot.

# Seared Tuna on Flatbreads with Wasabi

2 lb. of sushi-grade ahi tuna, sliced 1/8" thick
1 box of sesame flatbreads
1 C. arugula
1 jar of wasabi powder
½ C. olive oil
¼ C. soy sauce
2 cloves of garlic, minced
1 Tsp. dry mustard
3 Tbs. sesame seeds

In a medium bowl, add olive oil, garlic, soy sauce, dry mustard, sesame seeds and whisk together well. Marinate the sliced tuna in this mixture for 2 hours. On a large platter, lay out the flatbreads, side by side. Sprinkle the arugula over the tops of the flatbreads.

Grill the tuna on a hot grill for 2 minutes on each side. Place the grilled tuna on top of the arugula. Try to put one piece of tuna on each piece of flatbread.

Prepare the wasabi as directed on the jar. Add an extra teaspoon of water and drizzle over the top and serve.

# Memories of Past Parties

_____

_____

_____

_____

_____

_____

_____

_____

_____

_____

_____

_____

_____

_____

_____

_____

# Elegant Dinner Party #1

Serves 8
French Onion Soup au Gratin
Caesar Salad
Beef Tenderloin with Horseradish Cream
Twice-baked Potatoes
Steamed Baby Carrots with Tops and Haricot Vert (French Green Beans)
Homemade Strawberry Shortcake with Fresh Whipped Cream

This is my favorite menu for a dinner party of 8-12. It is sure to get rave reviews, however, it involves a four-hour preparation commitment. So, if you have the time, this one is a winner!

Here are some tips to make this a <u>no-stress</u> party.

- Make the onion soup the day before the party.
- Toast the croutons for the **soup** and the **salad**, the day before the party.
- Order tenderloin from your butcher or market the day before the party. I always use a butcher and I ask him to trim it up nicely.
- Set the table the day before or the morning of the party. (This is a good idea because you might have forgotten candles or napkin rings and it will give you time to get them)
- Make the horseradish cream the morning of the party.
- Make the twice-baked potatoes the night before or the morning of your party.
- Make the Caesar dressing the morning of the party. (It will taste much better.)

# Complete shopping list for Dinner Party #1

## Butcher
5 lb. beef tenderloin

## Liquor Store
Red wine (Cabernet)
Chardonnay

## Farm or Market
6 large Spanish or Vidalia onions
2 large lemons
12 large baking potatoes
1 garlic bulb
1 ½ lb. baby carrots w/tops
1 lb. haricot vert (French green beans)
1 package of fresh chives
3 heads of romaine lettuce
1 lb. of fresh strawberries
Fresh mint leaves (optional)
2 16-oz containers of sour cream
1½ lbs of butter
1 package of cream cheese
1½ pints of heavy cream
2 containers frozen strawberries with sugar
Olive oil
Kosher sea salt
Fresh ground pepper
Gruyere cheese
1 lb. grated parmesan cheese
1 loaf Italian Scali bread
1 loaf French bread
5 cans of beef broth
Bisquick

## Non-food items
Candles
Fresh Flowers

# French Onion Soup au Gratin

This recipe makes a lot of soup. I always take a third and freeze it for a snowy day.

5 or 6 large Spanish onions (Vidalias are great, too!)
4 cans of beef broth
1 stick of butter
3 cups of water
2 beef boullion cubes
1 Tbs. Gravy Master® (this will give your soup a nice, caramel color)
½ C. red wine
Salt and pepper
Gruyere cheese
French bread

Slice onions in 1/8-inch slices, after taking the skin off. Melt butter in a large saucepan on medium heat. Add onions to butter and lightly salt them, stirring around, making sure they all mix with the butter. Keep cooking until the onions are limp and almost translucent (at least 15-20 minutes). Add the beef broth, and then water. Drop in the bouillon cubes and add the red wine. Next, add the Gravy Master® and some salt and pepper.

Simmer your soup for about 2 hours. This soup tastes best when you serve it on the second day, so if this is your first course of an elegant dinner party, make it a day or two before.

Cut your French bread into 1½-inch slices and lightly toast on both sides, either in the broiler or a frying pan. Slice your Gruyere cheese with a cheese slicer or mandoline into very thin slices; you will use about 6 per crock.

Fill each crock with **hot** soup, place a piece of toasted bread on top, and lay the slices of cheese, covering the French bread. Broil these about 3-5 minutes, or until the cheese is melted and bubbly. (I do this on a cookie sheet so that the soup won't spill all over your oven)

# Traditional Caesar Salad with Homemade Croutons

2 heads of washed romaine lettuce
½ C freshly grated parmesan cheese
Ground pepper
Salt
**For the dressing:**
¾ C. olive oil
2 cloves of garlic, minced
2 Tbs. fresh lemon juice
4 Tbs. Worcestershire sauce
½ C. freshly grated parmesan cheese
1 egg, coddled (cooked for 1 minute in boiling water)

Note: if you wish to make an "eggless" dressing, substitute the dressing packet in a "Caesar salad in a bag" found in the produce section of the grocery store.

Salt and pepper

In a food processor, add oil, Worcestershire, lemon juice, minced garlic, and egg **or** the "in-a-bag" salad dressing. Mix well. Add salt and pepper and cheese. Mix again. The dressing tastes better if made 2-3 hours before serving. It separates, so you will need to mix it right before serving. Refrigerate, and then mix before serving.

**For the croutons:**
10 slices of scali bread (with seeds)
Olive oil
2 cloves of garlic, minced
Salt

In a large bowl, add oil and minced garlic. Cut the bread into 1½" pieces. Toss the bread pieces into the oil and garlic mix. In a large skillet or electric frying pan, toast the croutons on both sides.

Keep the heat low to medium or they will burn. Toast them until they are golden brown on each side.

In a large bowl, add romaine, grated cheese, and croutons. Gradually add the dressing (nobody likes a soggy Caesar. Add ground pepper. Serve on individual plates.

Note: If using romaine from a bag, you will need 3 bags.

Note: For a fancy touch, using a potato peeler, peel individual slices of parmesan for garnish.

# Roasting a Tenderloin

This is easy thing to make and it is always a hit (as long as you're not serving it to a vegetarian!).

You should calculate about one-half pound per person. So for 8 people, I would cook a 4-5 lb. tenderloin. (I sometimes add a little, just in case!)

Place the tenderloin in a large roasting pan and rub with ¾ Tbs. of kosher sea salt and freshly ground pepper.

Bake at 350° for 20 minutes per pound.

# Horseradish Cream Sauce

4 Tbs. prepared horseradish
5 Tbs. sour cream
2 tsp. freshly squeezed lemon juice
2 Tbs. fresh minced chives
Salt and pepper

Combine all ingredients, and season with salt and pepper, to taste.

# Twice-baked Potatoes

8 large baking potatoes
1½ sticks butter
1 16-oz. package of cream cheese
1 16-oz. container of sour cream
3 T. fresh, chopped chives
Paprika
Salt & pepper

Wash all the potatoes and bake them at 400° for 1 hour. While they are baking, combine butter, sour cream, and cream cheese together in a large, stainless steel bowl. Once the potatoes are baked, cut them in half, **lengthwise.** Scoop out the cooked potatoes and add to the butter and cheese mixture. (The hot potatoes will help soften the butter and cream cheese.) After you have created 12 potato shells, line them on a cookie sheet. Mix the other ingredients with an electric mixer until the lumps are removed and you have a smooth mixture. Stir in the chives.

Fill each shell with the potato mixture, and then drag a fork lightly to make "pretty" potatoes and place them back on the cookie sheet.

Give each one a light sprinkle of paprika.

Bake @ 375° for about 35 min. (until lightly browned)

## Tips on this recipe
If you're using this for an elegant dinner party, you can make these the day before to save time.

I like to fill a pastry bag with potatoes mixture and refrigerate for about 1 hour. For more decorative potatoes, stick chives in before serving.

# Strawberry Shortcake

3 C. Bisquick® baking mix
¾ C. milk
4 Tbs. sugar
4 Tbs. salted butter, melted
1 lb. fresh strawberries, washed & sliced
2 containers of frozen strawberries (with juice), thawed at room temperature
Fresh mint leaves
Homemade whipped cream

In a large mixing bowl, combine Bisquick®, milk, sugar, and butter. Mix well with a rubber spatula or gloves. Once a soft dough forms, lightly press into a 9"x9" glass baking dish. Note: This recipe is on the Bisquick® box and it tells you to drop spoonfuls on a cookie sheet for individual shortcakes. I like it better this way. If you are not baking these right away, cover with wax paper and refrigerate. Bake at 425° for about 15 minutes or until shortcake is golden brown.

Mix the fresh strawberries with the frozen strawberries; be sure to save 8 fresh strawberry halves for garnish with a mint leaf.

Cut the shortcakes and cover each on with plenty of strawberries and juice, a heaping dollop of whipped cream and garnish with a strawberry and mint leaf! This is delicious!

# Helpful Hints I learned while preparing this menu

_____

_____

_____

_____

_____

_____

_____

_____

_____

_____

_____

_____

_____

_____

_____

# Elegant Dinner Party #2

* Menu & Tips for a No-stress Party

* Complete Shopping List

*Pan-seared Scallops with Beurre Blanc Sauce

*Fancy Cucumber Salad with Balsamic Vinaigrette

*Fresh Lobster Casserole

*Horseradish Mashed Potatoes

*Broccoli & Tomato Medley

*Seasonal Berries with Fresh Whipped Cream

# Elegant Dinner Party #2

Serves 8
Pan-seared Scallops in a Beurre Blanc Sauce
Fancy Cucumber Salad with crumbled Feta & Balsamic
Vinaigrette
Fresh Lobster Casserole
Horseradish Mashed Potatoes
Broccoli Tomato Medley
Seasonal Berries with Fresh Whipped Cream

This is a wonderful menu for a summer party. The preparation for this menu is about 3 hours, however the only dishes that cannot be prepared the morning of the party are the scallops and the mashed potatoes (and, of course, the whipped cream).

Here are some tips to make this a <u>no-stress</u> party:

- Peel the cucumbers and "form" them the morning of the party.
- Chop all salad vegetables and store in Ziploc® bags, the morning of the party.
- Pick up lobster meat the day of the party. It must be FRESH!
- Prepare the stuffing the morning of the party.
- Make the broccoli & tomato medley the morning of the party.
- Wash and trim all berries and store in airtight Tupperware® containers.

# Complete Shopping list for Elegant Dinner Party # 2

## Fish Market
4 lbs. of fresh lobster meat (knuckles work best)
1½ lbs. fresh sea scallops

## Farm or Market
3 lemons
2 lbs. broccoli florets
6 heirloom tomatoes of tomatoes on the vine
Bunch fresh parsley
1 bermuda onion
3 shallots
2 heads of romaine lettuce
1 pint of grape tomatoes
6 large cucumbers
Garlic
2 medium onions
8 potatoes
1 lb. of fresh strawberries
1 pint of blueberries
1 pint of raspberries
1 pint of blackberries
Fresh mint leaves

## Liquor Store
White wine

## Grocery Store
1 container of prepared horseradish
Brown sugar
1 container of crumbled feta cheese
Dry mustard
Parmesan cheese
Milk
Ritz crackers®

Confectioner's sugar
1 package Cabot Sharp Cheddar Cheese®
Real vanilla extract
Butter
1 lb. unsalted butter
1 quart heavy cream
White vinegar
Balsamic vinegar
Olive oil

# Pan-seared Sea Scallops in a Beurre Blanc Sauce

For scallops:
2 lbs. of fresh sea scallops
1 fresh lemon
¼ C. clarified butter
Kosher sea salt
For Beurre Blanc Sauce:
2 Tbs. vegetable oil
¼ C. white vinegar
1 C. white wine
3 medium shallots (julienned)
½ C. heavy cream
3 Sticks of unsalted butter
1 Tbs. fresh lemon juice

In a colander, rinse scallops with cold water, then drain. Toss scallops with a squeeze of fresh lemon juice and about 1½ Tbs. of kosher sea salt. In a large skillet, add clarified, melted butter, and scallops, over medium heat. Watch them closely and turn each one with tongs or a small spatula, lightly browning each side. (About 3 minutes on each side.)

Place the browned scallops on a cookie sheet and set aside.

In a heavy saucepan, sauté the julienned shallots in oil until they become soft. Add white vinegar and white wine and reduce by half. Next, add heavy cream and reduce by half again. Turn heat to very low and add butter while whisking. Once the butter has completely melted, remove from heat, and strain the sauce into a bowl. Stir in lemon juice, and add salt and pepper to taste.

This recipe can be used as either a first course or a main course. Place a serving of scallops on each individual plate and drizzle with a couple of spoonfuls of sauce and serve.

# Fancy Cucumber Salad

5 or 6 large cucumbers
1 pint sweet grape tomatoes
1 medium Bermuda onion
2 heads of romaine lettuce, washed and "ripped" into small pieces
1 small can sliced black olives
1 block of feta cheese, cut into small cubes

Using a mandoline, slice the cucumber skin into long pieces. Save the pieces and roll up each slice. Place each roll into a Ziploc® bag and chill in the refrigerator until about 1 hour before your guests arrive. You will need about 4 slices to arrange a circle on each individual plate. Chop all ingredients into small pieces. (The key to this salad is to not use a knife.)

Assembly of the salads:

Take 8 individual salad plates and arrange the cucumber skins, on their sides, in a circle (about 5" or 6" diameter). Next, fill each "cucumber bowl" with chopped romaine, cubed cucumber, chopped tomatoes, chopped onions, olives, and chopped feta. Drizzle with balsamic vinaigrette and serve. This salad is something they will be talking about for days!

# Balsamic Vinaigrette

1 C. "good" olive oil
½ C. "good" balsamic vinegar
1 garlic clove, minced fine
1 tsp. dry mustard
4 Tbs. brown sugar
3 Tbs. water

Mix all ingredients in a cruet and shake well. This should be made at least 3 hours prior to serving.

# Fresh Lobster Casserole

1½ lb. freshly shucked lobster meat (knuckle meet works great!)
3 sleeves Ritz® Crackers, chopped fine in a food processor
1 stick butter
¼ C. white wine
1 medium onion, chopped fine
¼ C. fresh parsley, chopped fine
1 lemon

In a large skillet, melt butter on medium heat. Add onion and white wine and sauté until soft and translucent. Lower the heat and gradually add Ritz® cracker crumbs. Mix well. Sprinkle the parsley and mix into the stuffing. Remove from the stove.

In a glass casserole dish, spread out your lobster meat, covering the bottom of the dish evenly. Spoon the stuffing over the lobster meat, just lightly covering the lobster. It's best if some of the lobster is "peeking" out. Squeeze the juice of a small lemon over the top and bake about 25 minutes at 350. Serve with drawn butter if you wish, but, it's not necessary.

Note: This recipe can be prepared the morning of your dinner.

# Potato Gratin with Caramelized Onions

2 medium onions
2 Tbs. vegetable oil
6 potatoes
2 C. heavy cream
1 C. parmesan cheese
Salt and pepper

In a large skillet, heat the oil. Julienne the onion and add to the oil. Cook onion slowly until caramelized (turn dark brown), stirring occasionally. Peel the potatoes and slice them thin, using a mandoline. Add them to a large bowl. Next, add the cream, onions, cheese, and salt and pepper. Mix well and place them into a greased 9" x 12" baking pan. Cover with foil and cook for 1 hour at 350° for 1 hour. After 1 hour, remove the foil and cook for 15 – 20 minutes, or until the top is browned.

# Seasonal Berries & Fresh Whipped Cream

1 lb. of fresh, perfectly ripened strawberries, cut into bite size pieces
2 pints of fresh blueberries
2 pints of fresh raspberries
1 pint of fresh blackberries
Fresh mint leaves for garnish

Wash and gently dry all berries, be careful not to squish them. Lightly toss all berries into a large bowl and squeeze a little bit of fresh lemon over them and toss them again.

# Fresh Whipped Cream

1 Pint of heavy whipping cream
2 Tbs. confectionary sugar
1 Tsp. real vanilla extract

In a mixing bowl, beat all the cream on high for about 3 minutes. Sprinkle in the sugar and vanilla and beat on high again until the cream is fluffy and somewhat stiff. It is best to beat the cream right before use.

Take 8 individual martini glasses, and fill them with your mixture of fresh berries.

Put a big dollop of fresh whipped cream on top of each dessert and tuck a mint leaf into each dollop of whipped cream.

# Helpful Hints I learned while preparing this menu

_____

_____

_____

_____

_____

_____

_____

_____

_____

_____

_____

_____

_____

_____

_____

_____

_____

# Elegant Dinner Party #3

*Menu & Tips for a No-stress Party

*Complete Shopping List

*Spinach Salad with Maple Pecan Vinaigrette

*Pork Tenderloin encrusted with Panko and Dijon

*Potato Au Gratin with Caramelized Onions

*Homemade Applesauce

*Steamed Sugar Snap Peas

*Apple Crunch with Vanilla Ice Cream and Butterscotch Sauce

# Elegant Dinner Party #3

*Serves 8*

Spinach Salad with Maple Pecan Vinaigrette
Pork Tenderloin Encrusted with Panko and Dijon Mustard
Potato Au Gratin with caramelized onions
Homemade Applesauce
Steamed Sugar Snap Peas
Apple Crisp with Vanilla Ice Cream and Caramel Sauce

Here are some tips to make this a <u>no-stress</u> party.

- Prepare the tenderloin the morning of the party. This will save a lot of time.
- Prepare the dressing the morning of the party.
- Prepare the applesauce the morning of the party and heat right before serving.
- As always, set the table the morning of the party.
- This is a wonderful fall menu. Keep it festive and hollow out a couple of pumpkins and place a jar inside and fill with jewel-tone flowers!

# Complete Shopping List for Elegant Dinner Party #3

## Butcher
4 pork tenderloins (about 2 lbs. each)

## Liquor Store
Red wine (Merlot)
Chardonnay

## Farm or Market
12 Granny Smith apples
8 Idaho potatoes
2 lb. broccoli florets
6 large tomatoes (heirloom work best)
3 bags of baby spinach
1 Pint of yellow cheery tomatoes
Parmesan cheese
1 block of Cabot Sharp Cheddar Cheese®
1 lb. pecans, shelled & halved
Butter
Premium vanilla ice cream
Butterscotch caramel sauce
Prepared horseradish
Milk
Panko (Japanese breadcrumbs)
Dijon mustard (Stonewall Kitchen's Martini Mustard®)
Cinnamon
Nutmeg
Granola cereal with almonds
Light brown sugar
## Non-food items
Candles
Fresh flowers
Pumpkins (optional)

# Baby Spinach Salad with Maple Pecan Vinaigrette

Serves 8
6 C. baby spinach, washed and spun dry
1 Pint of yellow cherry tomatoes

In a large bowl, combine both ingredients and season with salt and pepper.

## Maple Pecan Vinaigrette

1 lb. of pecans, toasted
½ C. maple syrup
½ C. balsamic vinegar
1 C. extra virgin olive oil
Salt & Pepper to taste

Toast pecans on a cookie sheet at 350° for about 10 minutes. In a mixing bowl, add maple syrup, balsamic vinegar, and olive oil. Whisk together by hand. Add salt & pepper. Add the pecans and drizzle over the greens. Serve immediately.

# Pork Tenderloins Encrusted with Panko and Dijon Mustard

4 pork tenderloins, trimmed
2 C. panko breadcrumbs
6 T. "good" Dijon mustard. (Stonewall Kitchen's Martini Mustard® works well)
Salt and pepper
Oil

Salt the trimmed pork tenderloins and place on a plate. In a large skillet or an electric frying pan, heat 5 Tbs. of vegetable oil. Once the oil is hot, place the tenderloins in the pan and turn them every 2-3 minutes, browning all sides of the pork. Once they are browned, remove them from the pan and put them on a plate. Put the panko breadcrumbs on a separate plate and the Dijon mustard in a bowl. Using a pastry brush, cover each tenderloin with the Dijon mustard. Next, roll the pork in the panko breadcrumbs. The mustard will make the breadcrumb "stick." Place the pork in a large roasting pan. Bake at 375° for about 1 hour or until done.

# Homemade Applesauce

5/6 medium sized apples (Granny Smith work best)
3 T. sugar
4 T. water
Cinnamon (sprinkle)
Nutmeg (sprinkle)

Peel apples and slice into ¼-inch slices, then cut in half. Place the apples in a microwave-safe bowl and add water. Cover with plastic wrap and cook on high for 3 minutes in the microwave. Mash them together and add sugar. Cover and cook again for 2 minutes on high. Add a sprinkle of cinnamon and nutmeg if desired and serve.

# Horseradish Mashed Potatoes

8 Idaho potatoes, peeled
2½ sticks of butter
1 pint whole milk
4 Tbs. prepared horseradish
Salt and white pepper to taste

Boil potatoes until tender. Pour the potatoes into a colander and "steam out" for about 3 minutes. Heat milk and butter in a small saucepan to warm. Return the potatoes to the pot and mash them. Add milk and butter mixture and whip until smooth and creamy. Stir in horseradish and add salt and pepper to taste.

# Broccoli and Tomato Medley

4 C. of fresh, steamed broccoli
2 C. of diced, fresh tomatoes (heirloom or tomatoes on the vine)
1 stick of butter
¼ C. of fresh, grated parmesan cheese
1 block of Cabot Sharp Cheddar Cheese®, grated
Salt and pepper

In a bowl, dice tomatoes into small pieces and toss them with sea salt. This will make the tomatoes very juicy. Next, steam the broccoli until it turns bright green and slightly tender. Melt the butter and set aside. Grate the cheddar cheese with a hand grater (or a food processor) and set aside. In a large casserole dish, add steamed broccoli and cut into bite-sized pieces. Add salt and pepper. Pour on the butter and sprinkle with parmesan cheese. Spoon in the juicy tomatoes and mix gently. Sprinkle with cheddar cheese, and toss lightly. Bake at 375° for about 25 minutes or until the cheese is melted and it starts to bubble. This is so delicious and even better if you make it with garden tomatoes or heirloom tomatoes!

# Crunchy Apple Crisp

Serves 8
6 medium-size Granny Smith apples
1 C. flour
1 C. firmly packed light brown sugar
1 stick of butter, melted
1 T. cinnamon
1 T. ground nutmeg
1 C. granola cereal with almonds
Premium vanilla ice cream
Butterscotch caramel sauce (optional)

Peel and slice all the apples and place them in a greased glass baking pan (9" x 13"). In a large bowl, mix the flour, brown sugar, cinnamon, nutmeg, granola, and melted butter together. Sprinkle this mixture over the apples and bake for 30 minutes at 375°. The apples should be hot and bubbly. Serve with ice cream and caramel sauce. Yummy!

# Helpful Hints I learned while preparing this menu

_____

_____

_____

_____

_____

_____

_____

_____

_____

_____

_____

_____

_____

_____

_____

# Snowy Days and Quick Dinners

*Chicken Soup with Tomatoes

*Italian Sausages with Peppers and Pan-fried Potatoes

*Chicken Cordon Bleu

*Spaghetti Sauce

*Homemade Meatballs

*Veal Parmesan

*Eggplant Parmesan

# Chicken Soup with Tomatoes

1 whole chicken
1 bag of carrots
1 large bunch of celery
3 medium onions
4 cans chicken broth
2 cans of whole peeled tomatoes in juice
Baby bowties (pasta)

In pasta cooker (or a pot with strainer inside), fill halfway with cold water. Place 1 peeled carrot, 1 small onion (quartered), and the leaves of your celery. Take the whole chicken, rinse with cold water inside and out, and add it to the pot. Simmer the chicken for about 2 hours. (Do not boil.) Once the chicken is falling apart, the skin is very loose, and the meat is white, take the strainer out of the pot and place on a large plate. At this time, you can add the cut carrots, chopped onion, and celery to the pot with the chicken stock that was simmering for 2 hours. Pick apart the chicken, using all the meat you wish to add to your soup. (I use only white meat) Once you've dissected the chicken, discard the remaining wings, legs, body etc. Add the white meat to the soup. Open the 2 cans of tomatoes and pour into a bowl. Cut them up into pieces and add the tomatoes and the juice to the soup.

Simmer the soup for about 1 hour, or until all the vegetables are soft. In a small saucepan, cook the bow tie pasta until tender. DO NOT ADD ALL THE COOKED PASTA TO THE SOUP OR IT WILL SUCK UP ALL THE BROTH! I add about 2 tablespoons of cooked pasta to each serving of soup and then sprinkle with parmesan cheese. This soup is so good and very good for you!

Note: You can serve this soup with a simple salad and crusty hot bread for dinner on a cold day. It's delicious!

# Italian Sausages with Peppers and Pan-fried Potatoes

2 lbs. of fresh Italian sausages (Garlic & Cheese, Hot or
Sweet, or mix them)
2 green bell peppers (sliced into ¼-inch strips)
2 red peppers (sliced into ¼-inch strips)
5 medium potatoes (all-purpose or red bliss)
1/3 stick of butter
Salt and pepper

Peel and cut the potatoes into 1" or 2" pieces. In a 2-quart
pan, parboil the potatoes until slightly tender. "Steam out" the
potatoes in a colander. In a large skillet, add the butter and melt it
over medium heat. Add the potatoes and lightly salt them. Cook
and turn them, browning on all sides. This takes about half an
hour.

In an electric frying pan, cook all the sausages until browned on all
sides (about 15 minutes). Once they have browned, cut them up
into 2" slices. Put them back in the frying pan and add the peppers
and cover. Keep turning them, making sure they are thoroughly
cooked. Mix in the pan-fried potatoes and serve hot.

# Chicken Cordon Bleu

6 thinly sliced, trimmed chicken breasts
12 slices of imported ham, sliced thin
12 slices of Munster cheese
Flour
1 Tbs. butter
Salt
Pepper
Toothpicks (round)

Rinse chicken breasts in cold water. Onto a large plate, spoon about 1½ cups of the flour. Dip each piece of chicken into the flour lightly. In a large skillet, melt the butter on medium heat. Pan fry each piece of chicken about 2 to 3 minutes on each side (do not fully cook the chicken). In a glass baking dish, lay each piece of pan-fried chicken and put 2 pieces of ham and 2 pieces of cheese on top. Next, fold the chicken over and stick a couple of toothpicks to hold it together. Sprinkle a little salt and pepper over your finished chicken and bake for 25 minutes at 350°.

Note: This can be prepared earlier in the day. Just refrigerate before putting in the oven.

# Spaghetti Sauce

1 lb. ground sirloin
2 medium onions
3 cloves of garlic
10-15 fresh basil leaves
½ C. olive oil
½ C. fresh parmesan cheese (grated)
2 beef bouillon cubes
2 cans of Pastene® Ground Peeled Tomatoes
1 can Pastene® Tomato Puree
2 C. water

In a large saucepan, add olive oil and heat on medium heat. Using a food processor, chop the onions and add them to the pan. Next, mince the garlic using a garlic press. Cook onions and garlic for about 5 to 7 minutes, or until soft and lightly browned. Add the ground sirloin and mix well with the onions and garlic. Once the beef is nicely browned, add both cans of ground peeled tomatoes and tomato puree. Next, add water and stir together. Chop basil in the food processor or by hand with a knife. Add basil and fresh parmesan to the sauce, stirring occasionally. Drop in a beef bouillon cube. Cook for about 3 hours on low to medium heat.

# Italian Meatballs

2 lbs. of lean ground beef
3 cloves of garlic, minced
2 medium onions, chopped
2 eggs, beaten
2 C. of Italian breadcrumbs
½ C. fresh parsley, chopped
1 ½ C. freshly grated Parmesano Reggiano® cheese
½ C. milk

In a large mixing bowl, combine all the above ingredients in which the order they are listed. Mix well. You may want to use plastic gloves or sandwich baggies to really mix this up. After it is thoroughly mixed, make the meatballs. You can make them any size you like. I prefer to make them about 2" in diameter. This way they cook pretty quickly. In a large skillet or electric frying pan, cover the bottom with olive oil and turn heat to medium. Fry all the meatballs until they are browned on all sides. If you are not cooking these in spaghetti sauce after they have been browned, cut one in half to make sure they have been cooked through. Otherwise, drain them on a paper bag and drop them into a pot of freshly made spaghetti sauce and cook for another hour or so.

# Veal Cutlet Parmesan

8 fresh, thin-sliced veal cutlets
2 large eggs
¼ C. grated parmesan cheese
3 C. Italian-style breadcrumbs
Olive oil
12 slices mozzarella cheese
salt and pepper

Beat eggs in a shallow bowl and then beat in the parmesan cheese and set aside. On a large plate, pour on the breadcrumbs. Pound out veal cutlets on a countertop, using a meat pounder. This will make your veal very tender. Dip each cutlet into the egg and cheese mixture then into the breadcrumbs. After each one is evenly coated, set aside on a plate. In a large skillet or an electric frying pan, cover the bottom with olive oil and turn heat to medium. Fry each cutlet until nicely browned on each side (about 4 minutes on each side) and drain on a brown paper bag. Put the drained veal cutlets on a cookie sheet and place 2 slices of mozzarella on each cutlet. Bake at 375° for about 6-8 minutes, just until the cheese is melted.

Serve your veal on a plate with spaghetti and homemade sauce!

# Eggplant Parmesan

2 medium eggplants, peeled and sliced 1/8" thick
2 eggs, beaten
2 C. flour
3 Tbs. parmesan cheese
Salt & pepper
Olive oil
2 C. of freshly grated mozzarella

Combine beaten eggs and parmesan cheese in a shallow bowl.
Combine flour with salt and pepper on a plate. Using an electric
frying pan or a large skillet, cover the bottom with olive oil and heat
on medium. Dip each piece of eggplant into the egg-and-cheese
mixture, then the flour mixture. Then, put them into the pan and
brown each piece on each side. Drain each piece on brown paper
bags.

In a glass baking dish, put a thin layer of **meatless** spaghetti sauce.
Next, layer the cooked pieces of eggplant in the baking dish. You
should have about 4 layers when you are finished. Cover the top
with sauce, but not too much. Sprinkle with mozzarella and bake
at 350* until the cheese is melted and the bottom layer of sauce
is bubbling.

# My Favorite Quick Dinners

# Summer Cookout

*The Perfect Cheeseburger

*Hand-cut French Fries

*Bevy's Baked Beans

*Broccoli Salad

*Tri-colored Pasta Salad

# How to make the perfect cheeseburger

Makes 6 burgers

3 lbs. of ground sirloin (I only get this from my butcher)
Romaine lettuce, washed and dried
2 large tomatoes, garden or heirloom work best
1 Bermuda onion
American cheese
Real mayonnaise
Pepperidge Farm sesame seed hamburger buns

Shape sirloin into perfect half-pund patties. Fire up the grill! Grill burgers for 4 to 5 minutes on the first side, then flip. Lightly toast the buns while the burgers are cooking. After turning burgers, your buns should be ready. Spread a little mayo on the top half and then add a piece of romaine. Next, add a slice or two of juicy tomato and then a thin slice of Bermuda onion. After 3 minutes, add cheese to your burgers. Keep checking — make sure that the cheese is just melted, not brown. Place the burgers on a plate and let them sit 1 minute. Place the cooked burgers on the bottom of the buns and serve. Don't forget the ketchup!

# Hand-cut French Fries

8 large baking potatoes
4 C. vegetable oil
Kosher sea salt

In a large saucepan, add the oil and heat on medium. Peel each potato and cut lengthwise into slices (the size of steak fries). Then, place them into cold water. (Putting them in cold water will keep them from getting brown.) Once all the potatoes are cut, drain them and place them into the hot oil. They will cook for about 25 to 30 minutes. You want them to be brown and crispy. Don't move them around too much or they get mushy. Once they start to brown up, you can move them with some large tongs. Be careful: the oil is very hot. Once they are done, take them out with tongs and place them into a large paper bag. You might want to double the bag, so the oil doesn't leak.

Sprinkle on some sea salt and serve them hot with ketchup.

# Bevy's Baked Beans

3 cans of B&M Original Baked Beans®
1 medium onion, chopped
½ C. yellow mustard
1 C. light brown sugar

Pour the beans into a 2-quart casserole dish. In a medium bowl, mix the mustard with the brown sugar. Keep stirring until the mixture reaches a thick batter consistency. Pour it into the beans and stir well. Add the chopped onion and stir well. Bake at 375° for about 25-30 minutes, or until hot and bubbly.

# Broccoli Salad

4 C. of washed, trimmed broccoli florets (raw)
2 C. of shredded cheddar cheese
¼ C. bacon bits
1 C. shredded carrots
1 bottle of Hidden Valley Ranch® coleslaw dressing.
¼ C. chopped red onion

Toss all the above ingredients in a large bowl. Refrigerate for at least 3 hours.

# Pasta Salad

1 package of tri-colored rotini pasta
2 green peppers, cut into small pieces
1 small can of black olives, sliced
1 C. shredded carrots
1 C. sugar snap peas (raw)
1 small red onion, chopped into small pieces
1 package Good Seasons® Italian dressing, **prepared**
¼ C. parmesan cheese, grated fine

Cook and drain the pasta to desired tenderness, about 10 minutes. Toss with a little olive oil. Add all the vegetables and cheese. Use about half of the Italian dressing and refrigerate at least 3 hours before serving.

# Cookout Notes

# Aloha! Hosting a Hawaiian Luau

*How to Host a Hawaiian Luau

*Luau Cocktails

*Roasted Red Pepper Dip

*Salad with Pineapple-Orange Dressing

*Pineapple Chicken

*Rice Pilaf & Steamed Peapods

# How to host a Hawaiian Luau

Pick a date for your luau (preferably in the summertime).

Send out a festive invitation. Most stationery stores sell specific luau invitations.

Create a menu for your party. You may want to serve a dinner or cocktails and appetizers.

Once you've determined the number of guests, you need to decide on decorations.

I like to order luau decorations from Oriental Trading Company® (800 228-2269). They have a wonderful assortment of everything you will need such as:

Grass skirts
Hawaiian leis
Exotic drink glasses or cups
Paper drink umbrellas
Hawaiian tablecloths
Torches for your yard or pool
Luau music CDs
Party favors
Limbo games
Candles
Paper decorations

You will be able to find these things at your local party store as well, but the prices will be higher.

The only thing I have to say about an outdoor party is always have a plan B. By that, I mean it could rain. So, unless you have a covered deck or you rent a tent, you could have some wet guests or your party may have to be moved inside, so plan for that.

# Luau Cocktails

## Blue Hawaii
1 oz. light rum
1 oz. Blue Curacao
1 Tbs. fresh-squeezed lemon juice
1 oz. pineapple juice

Mix well and serve over crushed ice with a cherry and orange garnish.

## Planters Punch
1½ oz. light rum
½ oz. grenadine
1 tsp. Cointreau®
2 tsp. pineapple juice
½ oz. fresh-squeezed lemon juice
½ oz. fresh-squeezed lime juice
½ oz. sugar syrup
Splash club soda

Mix all ingredients except club soda. Shake with ice and strain into a hurricane glass. Top with a splash of club soda and garnish with a cherry and pineapple slice.

## Frozen Piña Colada
1½ oz. coconut cream
3 Tbs. crushed pineapple
1½ oz. light rum
1 C. crushed ice

Combine all ingredients into a blender. Blend on high until "slushy." Pour into hurricane glass and garnish with pineapple wedge and cherry.

# Roasted Red Pepper Dip

1 small onion, chopped
2 large garlic cloves, sliced
¼ C. olive oil
1 12-oz. jar of roasted red peppers
1/3 C. walnuts, toasted
1/3 C. basil leaves, packed
2 Tsp. fresh lemon juice

In a medium skillet, sauté onion and garlic in oil until soft. Add all other ingredients in a food processor and chop until walnuts are very small. Add the onion and garlic to the mixture in the food processor. Pulse a couple of times until all ingredients are blended together. Serve this dip with pita chips or soft pita.

# Salad with Pineapple-Orange Dressing

Mesclun greens
Radishes
Cucumbers
Red Onions
Tomatoes
Mix all the above ingredients in a large bowl.

# Pineapple Orange Dressing

½ C. pineapple chunks
1 can mandarin orange segments, drained
2 Tbs. fresh parsley, chopped
3 Tbs. fresh lemon juice
1 Tbs. vegetable oil
3 Tbs. honey
Salt & pepper to taste

In a food processor, combine all ingredients and puree. Chill for
at least 1 hour before serving.

# Pineapple Chicken

Serves 8
2 Tbs. butter
2 Tbs. olive oil
1 C. white flour
1 Tsp. salt
1 tsp. paprika
¼ tsp. fresh ground pepper
8 Boneless, skinless chicken breast halves
1 20 ounce can pineapple chunks in heavy syrup
½ C. sliced green pepper
2 scallions, sliced
1 Tbs. brown sugar
¼ C. dry sherry

Preheat oven to 425° f. In a shallow baking pan, melt the butter mixed with the olive oil in the oven. Mix flour, paprika, and salt and pepper in a large Ziploc® bag. Drop in each piece of chicken, one at a time, evenly coating each piece. Place the coated chicken breasts in the baking pan with the melted butter. Bake for 20 minutes, and then turn the chicken.

In a bowl, combine the pineapple, green pepper, scallions, brown sugar, and sherry, and pour over the chicken. Lower the heat to 375° and bake until the sauce thickens up and the chicken is golden brown (about 45 minutes).

# Rice Pilaf

1/8 box thin spaghetti
1 Tbs. butter
1 can chicken broth
1½ C. Minute Rice®

In a 2-quart saucepan, melt the butter over medium heat. Break the spaghetti into 1" or 2" pieces and add to the butter. Lightly brown the spaghetti, constantly stirring. Once the spaghetti is browned, add 1 can of chicken broth. When the chicken broth starts to boil, fill the chicken broth can with minute rice and add it to the pan. Stir it up and cover. Remove from the heat and let it sit for 5-7 minutes. Add 1 Tbs. of butter and fluff with a fork. Cover again until the butter melts and serve.

# Steamed Peapods

2 lb. of fresh peapods
4 Tbs. of butter
Salt & pepper

In a vegetable steamer, steam the peapods for about 6 minutes. DO NOT OVERCOOK! They should be bright green and a little bit crisp.

Serve these in a large bowl, add butter and season lightly with salt and pepper.

# Themed Party Ideas and Party Supply Websites

_____

_____

_____

_____

_____

_____

_____

_____

_____

_____

_____

_____

_____

_____

_____

_____

# Sunday Jazz Brunch

*Brunch Menu

*How to Host a Sunday Jazz Brunch

*Brunch Cocktails

*Traditional Eggs Benedict

*Baby Spinach Salad with Blue Cheese &
Raspberries

*Chulah French Toast

*Spinach & Tomato Quiche

*Cheesecake w/Strawberries

# Brunch Menu

Mimosas (made with freshly squeezed orange juice)
Spicy Bloody Marys
Chardonnay
Non-alcoholic punch
Coffee and tea
Seasonal fruit display with assorted cheeses and water crackers
Basket of assorted pastries, bagels, and rolls
Salad of baby spinach, pecans, fresh raspberries, and crumbled bleu cheese with raspberry vinaigrette
Traditional eggs benedict with hollandaise sauce
Crispy bacon
Link sausages
Challah french toast with orange slices, fresh raspberries, and powdered sugar
Beef tenderloin with horseradish sauce
Red bliss home fries
Vegetable medley of carrots, haricot vert and sugar snap peas
Cheesecake with strawberries

# How to host a Sunday Jazz Brunch

## What you need:

Bagels & cream cheese

Chafing pans and hotplates

Assorted breads and muffins

Jams & preserves

Individually wrapped butter pats

Fresh flower bouquets

Fresh fruit & berries

Assorted juices

Spring water w/lemon

Coffee/Tea

Candles

Sausage links

Linen tablecloths

Serving platters

Lean bacon

Baskets with linen napkins

Jazz CDs

Chardonnay

Champagne

## How to put it all together:

Decide on a place where you will be setting up your buffet. If you have an island in your kitchen and you don't need the extra counter space, that will work perfectly.

Here's a fun idea and it works well with a brunch buffet or any type of buffet you may be hosting: Cover the table with one tablecloth, then place some different-sized "boxes" or risers on top of the tablecloth. Make sure you leave at least 6" to 8" between each box. The number of boxes you need depends on the number of different platters or dishes you will be serving. Next, take the second tablecloth (identical tablecloths work best) and drape it over the boxes, covering the boxes but not entirely covering the first tablecloth. You have just created "layers" and this will make the presentation of your buffet table very attractive. Now, in between the boxes, you can place some candlesticks and fresh flower bouquets to "dress it up."

## Note: It is a good idea to do this the night before your brunch so that you can create a "seating arrangement" for your food. If you prepare this ahead of time, you will know exactly where everything is going. You can also place your baskets, plates, chafing dishes, etc. ahead of time.

# Spicy Bloody Marys

Makes 4 cocktails
6 oz. of premium lemon vodka (I prefer to use Grey Goose Lemon®)
24 oz. of V-8® vegetable juice
4 Tbs. of prepared horseradish
1 Lemon
Salt and pepper
Celery sticks
Dash of Tabasco®
Dash of Worcestershire sauce

Mix vodka, V8® juice, horseradish, Tabasco®, and Worcestershire together in a glass pitcher with ice. Squeeze in the juice of half a lemon. Add salt and pepper. Serve in chilled glasses with a piece of celery for a garnish.

# Mimosas

Good champagne
Freshly squeezed orange juice

Combine 3 oz. of champagne (or ½ full) and 3 oz. of freshly squeezed orange juice. Be sure to use champagne flutes when serving mimosas.

# Traditional Eggs Benedict

12 farm-fresh large eggs, poached
12 slices of Canadian bacon, cooked on both sides
6 English muffins, toasted (12 halves)
Fresh parsley, chopped fine

Line the bottom of a chafing dish with the toasted English muffins. Place one piece of cooked Canadian bacon on each muffin, then one poached egg on top. Spoon about 2 to 3 Tbs. of hollandaise sauce over each one and a sprinkle of fresh parsley. Very delicious!

# Hollandaise Sauce

1 Tbs. fresh lemon juice
2 Tbs. hot water
3 large egg yolks
½ C. butter, melted
Salt & pepper, to taste

Using a double boiler (or a metal bowl placed over hot but not boiling water), put the egg yolks in the boiler top (or the metal bowl) and beat with a whisk until smooth and creamy. Add the fresh lemon juice and gradually add the butter. Slowly add the hot water and salt and pepper. Keep whisking for about 1 minute and sauce should become thick. Serve immediately.

# Baby Spinach Salad with Raspberries and Bleu Cheese

3 packages of washed baby spinach
1 Pint of fresh raspberries
2 C. of shelled pecan halves
1 C. of crumbled bleu cheese

Combine all ingredients into a large salad bowl. Do not toss this salad, because the raspberries are very delicate.

# Raspberry Vinaigrette

½ C. olive oil
¼ C. raspberry vinegar
2 Tsp. tarragon leaves, crushed
1 Tsp. minced shallots
1 Tsp. sugar

Combine all ingredients in a cruet and shake well.

# Challah French Toast

1 Loaf of challah bread (sliced thick)
3 eggs
1 tsp real vanilla extract
¼ C. heavy cream
Butter
Fresh raspberries and orange slices for garnish
Powdered sugar

In a large, shallow bowl, mix eggs, cream, and vanilla extract. (You may want to beat for 1 minute with an electric mixer) Dip each piece of bread into egg mixture, moisten both sides, and set aside on a plate. In an electric frying pan, melt 1 Tbs. of butter. Once butter is melted and the pan is hot, fry each piece of bread until lightly browned on each side. Arrange each piece of French toast on a platter, sprinkle lightly with powdered sugar, and garnish with fresh berries and orange slices.

# Spinach and Tomato Quiche

1 bag of fresh spinach
4 medium tomatoes (heirloom or on the vine)
3 large eggs
1¼ C. heavy cream
½ tsp. ground nutmeg
1 C. cheddar cheese
1 Oranoke® Pie Crust
Preheat oven to 375˚.

Cook spinach and drain well. Set aside. Dice tomatoes and sprinkle with salt. Set aside. In a food processor, beat eggs, cream, nutmeg, and salt and pepper for 1 minute. Prick the pie crust with a fork on all sides and bake for 10-12 minutes, or until lightly browned. Pour egg and cream mixture into pie shell until ¾ full. Add spinach and spoon in tomatoes. Sprinkle with cheddar cheese and bake at 375˚ for 35-40 minutes.

Note: You may substitute a variety of ingredients for this if you prefer.

Some other combinations may be:

Broccoli and Cheddar (2 C. cooked broccoli & 1C. cheddar)

Asparagus and Tomato (1½ C. steamed asparagus & 1 C. tomatoes

Mushroom and Cheddar (2 C. sautéed mushrooms & 1 C. cheddar)

Ham and Bacon (1½ C. imported ham & 1C. cooked, crumbled bacon)

# Cheesecake with Strawberries

2 pkgs. of cream cheese (softened)
3 eggs
1 tsp. real vanilla extract
2/3 C. sugar
Frozen strawberries in juice (thawed)
Fresh strawberries, sliced

In a large bowl, using an electric mixer, beat the cream cheese until smooth. Gradually add the sugar and then the eggs, one by one. Once the mixture is very smooth, stir in the vanilla. Pour the mixture into a graham cracker crust and bake for 50 minutes at 325°. Chill the cheesecake for at least 2 hours before serving. Serve with 3 Tbs. of strawberry sauce on the bottom of the plate. Finish with a spoonful over the top with a few fresh strawberries. You may want to sprinkle a bit of powdered sugar over it as well.

You may use a prepared graham cracker crust or you can follow the following recipe and make one from scratch.

1¼ C. graham cracker crumbs
¼ C. Sugar
5 Tbs. melted butter
¼ Tsp ground cinnamon
¼ tsp. ground nutmeg

Mix all the above ingredients in a mixing bowl. Firmly pack the mixture into a 9" pie plate.

# Brunch Notes

# About the Author

Tracey Tonsberg found her "passion" when she started throwing parties and planning events. Princess in the Pantry was a great way to inspire her readers to entertain more often and simplify the entire process. Although Princess in the Pantry is her first book, she will be working on two additional titles, Pregnant Princess and Pampered Princess. Tracey is married and the mother of three. She and her family live in Kingston, MA

Printed in the United States
44305LVS00004B/103-255

9 781425 907402